Rose of Rumi...
petal 1

RHEA SINGH

BLUEROSE PUBLISHERS
India | U.K.

Copyright © Rhea Singh 2024

All rights reserved by author. No part of this publication may be reproduced, stored in a retrieval system or transmitted in any form or by any means, electronic, mechanical, photocopying, recording or otherwise, without the prior permission of the author. Although every precaution has been taken to verify the accuracy of the information contained herein, the publisher assumes no responsibility for any errors or omissions. No liability is assumed for damages that may result from the use of information contained within.

BlueRose Publishers takes no responsibility for any damages, losses, or liabilities that may arise from the use or misuse of the information, products, or services provided in this publication.

For permissions requests or inquiries regarding this publication,
please contact:

BLUEROSE PUBLISHERS
www.BlueRoseONE.com
info@bluerosepublishers.com
+91 8882 898 898
+4407342408967

ISBN: 978-93-6261-472-8

Cover design: Rishav
Typesetting: Rohit

First Edition: August 2024

Where u & i dissolve, there....
I'll meet you

~dedicated to moon, by his light

resisted & rose

resisted & rose

resisted & rose

Couldn't resist the feel thee outpoured

~thy Rose Rhea

Foreword...

The moment heard thy keys, couldn't resist that unknown feel
Now questioning what this is,
In journey of seeking thee within
Felt walking alone in this walk be,
Came across moon petals scattered on Earth we see
Started gathering our petals from our abode moon be
Will soon find petals 1200 forming me Rose of thee
Rumi

~thy rose Rhea

*Come with me in this journey of collecting beading petals,
     forming Rose of Rumi …*

1200 petals forming a Rose
~thy Rose

Moonlight Serenade

~thy beloved Cynthia

Acknowledgement...

This work of art, got rose within me, this rose, via longing moon, of this light. The love for moon, the deep intense unavoidable devotion towards moon, has made me write Rose of Rumi.

I would purely acknowledge my moon, o' love, my beloved, o' thee, to make me write this timeless piece of love for thee.

I thank moon, for bringing out the best from me, for strengthening me & instilling me with deep faith & confidence, & courage to walk on this unknown sand be.

Thanking lord of my heart...nd

thy rose Rhea

petal 1

drowning in those eyes, so moonchild
dissolved myself, o' beloved delight
o' dream, o' sweet, o' lovely, my beat
thy smile lightens, thy lady by the Sea

petal 2

o' thee lovely human
see the garden of deceit
deceiving thy inner being
open thy eyes
sync deep... sleep in
the flow of each being

petal 3

*Come take me to a place
where we together, smile in the . . .
Symphony of our moonlight*

petal 4

Swept by sorrow, a heart shines clean
Soul sounds denser, diamond thee seem

petal 5

*where, time fails
there lies our abode ... o' moon*

petal 5

*where, time fails
there lies our abode ... o' moon*

petal 6

wooing moon, worshipping you
a story breathing thousand years in me you

petal 7

*Cleanse thy heart of beliefs thee instilled
forget thyself in thee conscious feel
as thee a shell, manifesting love of Supreme*

petal 8

Wonderful, o' wonder
lovely, o' lover
thy presence mere
kisses my breaths dear

petal 9

*when you talk to me, o' sweet
thee get me confused to listen or to breathe*

petal 10

realised Realisation,
dissolving all phantoms of the garden of deceit

petal 11

Sometimes it feels painful a bit
at times, so lovely & sweet
this pleasureful pain
let our moonlight glisten a little bit

petal 12

*those dimples,
steal my soul*

petal 13

all that you need
a lens of wise be
as sight of consciousness
transcends sight of all feel

petal 14

I was sitting beside the seaside
of an icy frozen lake
when you came sat beside me
ice melted, started flowing as water
(where the lake symbolises my heart...
my sweetest heart)

petal 15

I was resting so happily on my sea bed
thee woke me up surface, the keys thee played
I resisted & rose,
resisted & rose,
resisted & rose,
couldn't resist the feel thee outpoured
chased reached up thee keys sea shore
found thee standing with elegance & grace thee wore

***petal* 16**

those eyes, thee still sea deep
A conscious play in between thy letters resonates thy being

petal 17

*not the material for which the world been played
it's the heart for which the Divine waits*

petal 18

as the night passes by
lets be closer with no why
as I myself don't know why
to tell you why. . .

petal 19

Fear not the pain
as thence thee experience
embrace it vulnerably
as these Reason thy existence

petal 20

we are sailing on same ship called moon,
where no one can interrupt our peace & feel

petal 21

Quantum Entanglement
or be it yin yang
no matter what its name is
lets remain one beyond time span
I may be wrong
let me be wrong
there's no harm in this,
it's in river form
let me be thy yin
you be my yang
lets together flow in the flow of this divine dance

petal 22

Ignorance cages you
Chains you...
to the deceitful garden of greed, where...
everything an illusion
an illusion,
blinding our source of being

petal 23

seek shelter
to those who disowns shelter
as they, sleep under the divine shelter

petal 24

*a timeless Romance
within us. . . a divine dance*

petal 25

Eyes tell as it is
Ears show the worlds of myths
connect with eyes
language, no need

petal 26

like taste to fruit
fragrance to flowers in bloom
thy purpose thee human, prospers you

petal 27

      in the sweet shining water
      shimmers the lord's beauty
with elegance & grace. . . mercy thee embody

petal 28

when mind & body seems dust on thy soul
thee under the clear sky of heaven, behold

petal 29

Blinded by greed
Deafened by extended needs
human fails to perceive
the sweetest silence
harmonising us free

petal 30

after fierce winter,
comes the lovely breeze
Cherry blossoms
thee bud beam ecstasy

petal 31

Silent & Still, those eyes appeal to me
lost in those rose garden, beautifully they plead

petal 32

*an honoured guest, a thought came
welcome wisely, thy worth it proclaims*

petal 33

you search for gem in world of vain
thee treasure is hidden, inside you gem. . .

petal 34

a flow,
so Ceaseless...
yea, ceaseless it seems
seemingly ceaseless it feels...
one full moon night
realised got dissolved
dissolved somehow
found got painted in thou
now
wish to immerse
immerse deep...
deep in those eyes, o' dream
wish not
not to wake from dream, o' sweet
wish,
wish only
moonlight to breathe...

petal 35

Zoomed out of time...saw
a castle been created
on the flagships thence conquered
by the strength thee instilled
o' dear moon of this light
then felt
a sudden nostalgia
thought...
how lovely this Cynthia castle shine
by the touch of thee grace
found myself longing...
only waiting
for the keys thee played...

petal 36

Dews glistening thy lips
kisses my soul, when I see...

petal 37

dive deep in the sea of awakening
surrender thyself in the journey of thee to thee
unleashing

petal 38

when you near me, you are moon
when you far away, moon is you

petal 40

Despite getting hurt each time
why these eyes can't comprehend thee wrong,
anytime

petal 41

Discretion dissolves all discrete
love flows beyond bounds, uniting you me

petal 42

in the garden of love, o' love
our roses bloom in thy love

Fragrance of thy sweet smile
Swoons my heart, dear dove

sweet melody of thy presence
mesmerises my eyes, sweetest love

petal 43

*that smile...
blooms me Rose*

petal 44

if not light
then, who will keep alive...
Sanctity of our moonlight

petal 45

*heaviness of heart evaporated
when rain of thy love percolated*

petal 46

let thy senses be courtiers to mind
let these sights obey thy might
when they dream in awakened eyes
then opens, gate to Divine

petal 47

Seek the knowledge from within
Soak in that wisdom of beam
thence enlighten, thee within

petal 48

*illusion drains the Sap of life from each
all fades, mere Consciousness breathes...*

petal 49

speak without words
hear words of no words
sweet Silence, the quest & quench to all thy
melancholic thirst

petal 50

look into the eyes of the lifelong traveller
the world seems small concise in him
as his wisdom, seemingly embraced...universe in him

petal 51

in the garden of thy belief
sweep withered leaves
sow thy gratitude seeds
thence patience, joy thee reap...

petal 52

Wish heaven takes my breaths, while asleep
as only dream unites me thee, o' dream

petal 53

Beauty of thee sea, under moonlight, those eyes
    Calms my sense of soul to ultimate delight

petal 54

*looking into those eyes, as if
looking into mine...so Reflective*

petal 55

let thee mirror reflects god's beauty
for thee, let love be... heavenly pretty

petal 56

Kiss not the shell
Kiss the soul
love resides inside
o' beautiful thee soul

petal 57

*board on boat of those
who sail to the Supreme
as they navigate by
the grace of light pristine*

petal 58

an innocent girl was playing in the field
her eyes twinkled bliss, drenched in ecstasy

petal 59

be humble like dust
bend bow surrender & trust
thy innocence glistens thy pristine worth

petal 60

Knowing divine
Escaping fear dying

petal 61

Cry deep
as much as you feel
empty clean,
o' crystal thee gleam

petal 62

o' moon
what shall I do
in this world of unknowns
I miss you

petal 63

Source of wind, unseen
seen by some, those wise perceive
with the eyes of realisation
thee bird fly free

petal 64

let not, I bloom in the garden of deceit
let not, I walk in the shadow of selfish meets
let prosper I in I of self feel
let prosper I in I uniting you me

petal 65

Have faith
Bow deep
to the ultimate light, the guide in thee
as everything fades
except the union to self in thee

petal 66

Hold my hand,
let me take you to
the densest forest of love, inside my heart
where a girl is hiding...
when the moonlight falls on her eyes of her inner
shy
Sweet moonlight, reflects the cry of her inner why
the why that..
that she feels that...

petal 67

Once wise advised
Embrace good & bad alike
as the divine guides
to thy self reflecting light

petal 68

o' the shooting stars
beseech thee, I humbly be
make moonlight together be
o' heavenly stars
bring back my moon to me
end this period of eclipse be
me merely longing my moon sweet...

petal 69

Where you & I dissolve, there... I'll meet you

petal 70

Need, the cause of all breathe
the moon, the mountain, the tree
all from nature's womb be
without reason, no one meets

petal 71

World walks outside to seek wisdom
Close thy eyes, its inside, the reason

petal 72

trust not the world
a mere garden of deceit
thee may get deceived
by the illusion it appeals

petal 73

Eyes of child see the wish of now
Eyes of wise see the need of now
wise sees to the end
whilst child lost in now then

petal 74

in the world of mirror
thee reflect thy inner
dust off the separation
dwell in divine union

petal 75

Fleeting, deceitful the pleasure appeals
drags you miles & miles, away from thy true being

petal 76

taste of divine wonder
leaves you bewilder
only wish you ponder
to tune in melody of the Supreme lover

petal 77

unlearn what you learnt
these words mere
burden thy peace dear...

petal 78

I see you smile, I smile too
I see you cry...I'm crying too
a drop of cry from your eye
make my heart dry die
in each water so thy
in each pristine so you, my hue
my heart shatter embraces each you

petal 79

I respect you more
than I respect myself
is it called love
I don't know myself

petal 80

o' moon
how thy light breathe,
when you afar.. my breaths too leave

petal 82

*I bow to you
sometimes Cresent ... sometimes Full*

petal 83

o' moon
I'll wait for the dawn to dawn
amidst the dews of which
I worship thee lord of my heart

petal 84

o' moon
thee love set me free
strengthens me complete
I thank thee
thy sweet smile
I live thee
as wind blows by
I wish thee
my soul cries...

petal 85

Blow off the clouds of desire
Behold the beam of selfless attire

petal 86

Joy reappears by fearing not the fear of fear...

petal 87

material confined to world's jurisdiction
this flow, abides by the love perception

petal 88

a promise,
light moon...moon light
moon moon... light light
in you
. . .
blue you
you hue
hue blue
me you

petal 89

o' moon
wish that warmth, within those arms
without you, light lost her charm...

petal 90

*Beyond cause & effect
a melody still connects…
of that Realm unclaimed
nothing can be proclaimed…*

petal 91

like the labour pain worth bearing
the journey of gestation, worth cherishing
likewise,
this life... worth longing

petal 92

*Been constantly formed
a wave dies, returns to the sea
so do the human, to the Supreme
play of time frame, you see...*

petal 93

*thee blossom in the garden of Supreme
o' thee fragrance, the love dissolving each*

petal 94

light whispered to her moon
handle me gently...

petal 95

o' wisdom
sadly thee, visitor in journey of each
seldom welcomed, in adversity of peace
where thee, the temple in every being

petal 96

*I wish to feel breathe a night
in which thy eyes breathe mine*

petal 97

Kingdoms change, people went & came
generations upon generations
Essence of wisdom & justice sounds same...

petal 98

*thee acquaintance help me found
"pleasure in pain"...*

petal 99

world says... god is love
I feel.. love is god
meaning same... Experience different

petal 100

*those who dwell in the voice of Stillness
bathes in the truth of Consciousness...*

thy rose re..uh

www.ingramcontent.com/pod-product-compliance
Lightning Source LLC
LaVergne TN
LVHW041703070526
838199LV00045B/1180